WHAT DO YOU KNOW ABOUT

GETTING INTO TROUBLE OR CRIME

PETE SANDERS and STEVE MYERS

COPPER BEECH BOOKS
BROOKFIELD, CONNECTICUT

Contents

© Aladdin Books Ltd 1996

All rights reserved

Designed and produced by
Aladdin Books Ltd.
28 Percy Street
London W1P 0LD

First published in
the United States in 1999 by
Copper Beech Books,
an imprint of
The Millbrook Press
2 Old New Milford Road
Brookfield, Connecticut
06804

Printed in Belgium

Designer   Tessa Barwick
Editor   Alex Edmonds
Illustrator   Mike Lacey
Picture   Brooks
Research   Krikler
                Research

**Library of Congress
Cataloging-in-Publication Data**
Sanders, Pete.
Getting into trouble or crime /
Pete Sanders and Steve Myers.
p. cm. — (What do you know
about)
Summary: Explains how and why
young people get into trouble, why
some people break the law, and
how to avoid getting into
troublesome situations.
ISBN 0-7613-3264-2 (lib. bdg.)
1. Juvenile delinquency Juvenile
literature. 2. Disorderly conduct
Juvenile literature. 3. Youth—
Conduct of life Juvenile literature.
[1. Juvenile delinquency.] I. Myers,
Steve. II. Title. III. Series: Sanders,
Pete. What do you know about.
HV9069.S248 1999   99-23034
364.36—dc21   CIP

5 4 3 2 1

HOW TO USE THIS BOOK

The books in this series are intended to help young people to understand more about personal issues that may affect their lives. Each book can be read by a child alone, or together with a parent, caregiver, teacher, or helper, so that there is an opportunity to talk through ideas as they come up. Issues raised in the storyline are explored in the accompanying text, inviting further discussion.

At the end of the book there is a section called "What Can We Do?" This section provides practical ideas that will be useful for both young people and adults, as well as a list of the names and addresses of organizations and helplines providing further information and support.

−1− *Introduction*

"I just thought we were having fun. I knew what we were doing was wrong, but I didn't think it was a big deal."

Most young people believe that they will never be in serious trouble. Despite this, the number of people involved in crime is on the increase. This book will help you to understand more about the law and some of the pressures facing young people. Each chapter introduces a different aspect of the subject, illustrated by a continuing storyline. The characters in the story have to deal with situations that many young people might experience. By the end you will know why some people end up breaking the law and understand how to make sure you don't put yourself in the same situation.

YEAH. BUT YOU CAN'T SAY ANYTHING. YOU DON'T KNOW ALEC. HE'S NOT JUST A RACIST OR A BULLY. I THINK HE GETS A KICK OUT OF HURTING PEOPLE. IF HIS BROTHER HADN'T BEEN THERE WITH ME...

HEY, WATCH OUT!

Growing Up

Growing up should be an exciting time. As you get older, you will be making choices about the way you want to live your life. You will be coming to terms with both the physical and emotional changes that puberty brings. Some of the pressures these produce may be hard to handle. There will also be outside factors to consider that may influence the decisions you make.

The progression from child to adult is full of new experiences.

One of the most important things you develop as you grow up is your sense of what is right and wrong. You learn that there are laws that everyone is expected to obey. If you break one of these laws, you may commit a criminal offense. But you also develop your own values and attitudes, based on how you feel about yourself and toward other people and the society you live in. Different people have different views. Some may try to persuade you to go along with something that you don't feel comfortable with. It is vital to be able to see when this is happening to you and be able to resist. This is particularly important if you know that what you are being asked to do is wrong or illegal.

▽ School had finished for the holidays. Todd Schaeffer and his friends were on their way home.

> A WHOLE SUMMER BEFORE WE'RE BACK AT SCHOOL. IT'LL BE GREAT, RASHID!

> WHAT ABOUT NEXT SEMESTER, THOUGH, WHEN WE ALL HAVE TO START NEW SCHOOLS? YOU WON'T EVEN BE GOING TO THE SAME ONE AS US, WILL YOU, CHARLIE?

> THAT'S RIGHT. AT LEAST YOU THREE WILL BE TOGETHER. I WON'T KNOW ANYONE.

▽ As they turned the corner, Charlie saw Todd's sister in the distance.

> HEY, TODD, ISN'T THAT DINAH? WHO'S SHE WITH?

> OH, SHE'S STARTED THIS STUPID GANG WITH JILL AND SOME OTHER FRIENDS OF HERS. THEY CALL THEMSELVES "THE WANNA-BES." CAN YOU BELIEVE IT?

> SHE DOESN'T LOOK PLEASED TO SEE YOU, TODD!

△ Roger was right. Dinah saw the boys and headed off in the other direction.

▽ The following weekend, Todd and the others went around to Rashid's house.

> DAD'S WORKING, SO WE CAN'T STAY IN THE HOUSE. LET'S HAVE A BALL GAME OUTSIDE.

> YES! DO YOU WANT TO JOIN IN, SHOBU?

> NO, THANKS. BY THE WAY, ROGER, WHAT'S GOING ON WITH ALEC? UMRAN WAS TALKING ABOUT HIM EARLIER. HE SAYS HE'S BEING A REAL PAIN.

▽ Umran was Rashid and Shobu's older brother.

> YOU SHOULD HAVE HIM AS A BROTHER! IF I WERE UMRAN, I'D TRY TO STAY AWAY FROM HIM. ALEC LIKES TO BULLY PEOPLE. HE'S GOT A REALLY VIOLENT TEMPER.

> I CAN'T BELIEVE THE TWO OF YOU ARE RELATED.

▽ The boys started their game.

> OKAY, RASHID, I'M GOING TO GET YOU WITH THIS ONE!

▽ Todd threw the ball, and Rashid hit a wild shot.

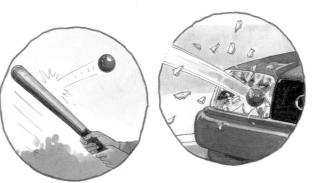

The boys ran off as the ball smashed the △ headlight of a neighbor's car.

DO YOU THINK HE SAW US?

I DON'T KNOW. BUT LET'S NOT STICK AROUND TO FIND OUT. IT'S ONLY A HEADLIGHT ANYWAY.

LET'S GO AROUND TO MY PLACE JUST IN CASE.

THERE'S NOTHING GOING ON IN THIS STUPID TOWN, AND EVERY TIME I TRY TO HAVE SOME FUN, YOU LAY DOWN THE LAW. WELL, I'M GOING TO MEET MY FRIENDS ANYWAY, AND YOU CAN'T STOP ME!

▽ When they arrived, Dinah and her mom were arguing.

YOU ALWAYS DO THIS TO ME. I'M SIXTEEN YEARS OLD, NOT TWO. I ONLY WANT TO MEET MY FRIENDS TONIGHT. I WON'T BE ON MY OWN AND I WON'T BE LATE. OKAY?

THAT'S NOT THE POINT, DINAH. I DON'T LIKE YOU JUST HANGING AROUND TOWN, ESPECIALLY AT NIGHT. I'M NOT HAPPY ABOUT THIS GANG OF YOURS, EITHER.

▽ When Rashid eventually got home that evening, he had a surprise waiting for him.

RASHID, JUST IN TIME. THIS IS MR. JEFFREYS. HE TELLS US YOU HAD TO FINISH YOUR GAME IN A HURRY TODAY AND LEFT YOUR BALL BEHIND.

OH, LOOK, I'M REALLY SORRY, MR. JEFFREYS. WE WERE JUST HAVING FUN. IT WAS AN ACCIDENT, HONESTLY. THINGS JUST GOT OUT OF HAND.

△ Dinah stormed out and went up to her room.

WHAT WERE YOU DOING, RASHID? PLAYING BALL IN A STREET WITH CARS EVERYWHERE!

APOLOGIZE AGAIN, AND GO UP TO YOUR ROOM. WE'RE ALREADY PAYING FOR A NEW HEADLIGHT, SO YOU CAN FORGET ABOUT THE NEW COMPUTER GAME YOU WANTED.

SORRY. WE DIDN'T DO IT ON PURPOSE. WE JUST PANICKED.

I KNOW THAT, BUT IT DOESN'T EXCUSE YOUR RUNNING AWAY.

▽ That night, Dinah sneaked out to join her friends.

I DON'T CARE IF I GET GROUNDED FOR THIS. I'M SICK OF MOM INTERFERING WITH EVERYTHING I DO. WHAT DID YOU TELL YOUR PARENTS, ZOE?

I DID THE SAME AS JILL AND SHAWNA. WE EACH TOLD OUR PARENTS WE WERE GOING OVER TO THE OTHER'S HOUSE.

I SUPPOSE THAT MEANS NO ONE REALLY KNOWS WHERE WE ARE!

young people to get together socially. They might feel bored, even angry. Often, the feeling that life is not working out the way they wanted has tempted some people into crime. It is as though they think they have nothing to lose. But, getting into trouble and crime will only make a bad situation worse.

DINAH'S MOOD HAS CAUSED HER TO ARGUE WITH HER MOM.

During puberty, you undergo major changes. Many of these are physical, as your body prepares for adulthood. There will also be significant emotional changes, as you begin to experience new feelings and ideas. Mood swings are common during this period. However, it is important not to let sudden rushes of feeling influence your actions and make you do something you might later regret.

RASHID AND THE OTHERS HAVE LET THEIR GAME GET OUT OF HAND.

What happened was an accident, but it may also have been a crime if they were thoughtless or ignored an obvious risk of damage to the car. Everyone likes to have fun. Enjoying social occasions with friends is a necessary part of life. However, your happiness should not be at other people's expense.

MANY YOUNG PEOPLE LIKE DINAH ARE PESSIMISTIC ABOUT THEIR FUTURE.

The conditions some live in, or their prospects for future employment, have sometimes led them to believe that their life will never change for the better. Some communities provide few, if any, opportunities for

—3— Trouble and Crime

It is a fact that crime is a part of life in our society. This doesn't make it acceptable, and we all have a duty to fight it.

Though the law itself is fairly clear about what is and isn't a crime, it is not always easy to know yourself whether what you are doing is a criminal offense. Everybody has been in trouble at some time or another. Perhaps you've not arrived home by an agreed deadline, or maybe you've been caught skipping a class at school and been told off. Though none of these are crimes, sometimes some of the things people do can cross the line between getting them into trouble and breaking the law.

There are many different kinds of crimes — such as those against the person, like assault or abuse, and those against property, such as theft or vandalism. All crime is unacceptable, but certain crimes are more serious than others. This means that the punishment for some offenses is more severe than for others. In some cases, people end up breaking the law without meaning to. Others know that what they are doing is a criminal offense. In some circumstances, knowingly going along with someone else who is committing a crime, or encouraging someone to break the law, may be crimes in themselves. That is why it is important to understand what the consequences of your actions might be.

Young people may find crime a hard habit to break, especially if they believe they are getting away with something.

▽ Soon the new term had arrived.

HEY, I'M NOT LOOKING FORWARD TO THIS EITHER, BUT THERE'S NO NEED TO LOOK SO MISERABLE.

NO, IT'S NOT THAT. WE WERE BURGLARIZED LAST NIGHT. WE ALL WENT TO THE MOVIES, AND WHEN WE GOT BACK, THE HOUSE WAS A MESS.

THE TV, VCR, AND STUFF. BUT THEY WENT THROUGH EVERYTHING. MOM SAID THAT WAS THE WORST PART – KNOWING THEY'D BEEN THROUGH HER THINGS.

WHAT? THAT'S AWFUL. WHAT DID THEY TAKE?

I KNOW. MY GRANDMA WAS BURGLARIZED A FEW YEARS AGO. SHE WAS NEVER HAPPY IN HER HOUSE AFTER THAT. SHE FELT FRIGHTENED AND AS THOUGH SOMEONE HAD MADE THE PLACE DIRTY.

WELL, WELL, IF IT ISN'T THE LITTLE PEOPLE READY TO JOIN THE BIG SCHOOL. HEY, ROG, I THOUGHT I TOLD YOU ABOUT MIXING WITH SCUM LIKE THIS.

◁ Roger's brother butted in.
▽ Todd and Rashid were now buddies with Dean.

I DON'T WANT TO GO STRAIGHT HOME TONIGHT. WHY DON'T WE GET SOMETHING TO EAT?

YOU MEAN THE SAME WAY WE DID YESTERDAY? THAT WAS A LAUGH.

LEAVE US ALONE. WE HAVEN'T DONE ANYTHING TO YOU.

COME ON, ALEC. CALM DOWN. WE WERE JUST TALKING.

WHAT DOES EDDIE MEAN? WHAT'S FUNNY ABOUT EATING?

I'VE NO IDEA. BUT DEAN COMES UP WITH SOME WILD IDEAS. I'M GLAD HE'S OUR FRIEND.

▽ They came to a shop. Shobu stayed outside, and the others went in.

▽ Outside, Todd was not pleased with Dean.

DEAN! WHAT ARE YOU DOING?

SHHH! DO YOU WANT US TO GET CAUGHT? JUST ACT NATURALLY – EDDIE'S GOT HIM OCCUPIED. WE DO THIS ALL THE TIME. LIVE DANGEROUSLY. IT'S FUN!

OH, COME ON, WE'RE NOT DOING ANY REAL HARM. THEY CAN AFFORD IT. RELAX, IT'S NOT A BIG DEAL.

SHOPLIFTING'S A CRIME, DEAN. MY WALKING OUT WITH THAT STUFF IN MY POCKET MAKES ME AS GUILTY AS YOU.

I CAN'T BELIEVE THIS. WHY DIDN'T YOU SAY ANYTHING?

I WAS JUST SHOCKED. I SHOULD HAVE SAID SOMETHING, BUT THEY COMMITTED THE CRIME.

ROGER AND HIS FAMILY WERE BURGLARIZED.

Every crime has a victim. The victim may be the community as a whole having to live with the results of crime. If people considered the effects on others and the upset that crime can bring, they might realize how wrong their actions are.

DEAN AND EDDIE HAVE SHOPLIFTED BEFORE AND NOT BEEN CAUGHT.

Sometimes one of the reasons people give in to the temptation to commit a crime is that they believe they can get away with it. Apart from the fact that this is no excuse for breaking the law, the reality is also very often different from the idea. Few people get away with a crime, and even if they do, it's unlikely they will do so the next time. Also, most people find it hard not to tell someone about what they have done.

CASE STUDY:
VITO, AGE 15

"Kids at school liked me because I was tough. There was one boy I was always picking on. I thought he was a wimp. I never really hurt him, just pushed him around — I knew it was wrong. One day the principal found out what was going on. She told me the other boy's work was affected and he was afraid to come to school. I was suspended for a while. I began to realize how the other kids only looked up to me because they were afraid of me. They weren't really my friends."

−4− Influences on Your Actions

"I used to blame my friend, because she started it, but I realized that I didn't have to go along with her. It was my decision, and I had to deal with any unpleasant consequences."

There is no one kind of person who gets into trouble or crime. Potentially it can happen to anyone. Influences on your thoughts and actions are all around you when you are growing up. Many young people who have been involved with crime have singled out reasons such as family background, dissatisfaction with their lives, or pressure from other people. These can all be very real motives. Even so, they are not excuses to break the law.

When you become a criminal, you risk damaging your own self-respect, reputation, and future prospects.

People's reasons for deciding to commit an offense may vary greatly. Some crimes are committed on the spur of the moment, either because the opportunity presents itself, or because a person becomes angry or upset and, for instance, lashes out at another person. Some people are jealous of others' success or possessions. Others believe that committing a crime will solve a particular problem. Sometimes, people are charmed by what they see as a glamorous side to crime. They may think other people will look up to them or believe that their lifestyle will be improved by breaking the law.

▽ A few weeks later, Dinah and her mom were arguing again.

DO YOU DO THIS TO UPSET ME? WHERE ARE YOU GOING DRESSED LIKE THAT?

WHAT'S WRONG WITH MY CLOTHES? IT'S NOT ILLEGAL TO LOOK GOOD, IS IT? I'M GOING TO A PARTY AT ZOE'S.

NOT LOOKING LIKE THAT, YOU'RE NOT, YOUNG LADY.

WE DON'T LIKE HAVING TO PLAY THE HEAVY-HANDED PARENTS, DINAH, BUT YOU DO TRY US SOMETIMES. WHEN YOU SNEAKED OUT LAST TIME, WE HAD NO IDEA WHERE YOU WERE.

I WAS FINE.

BUT WE DIDN'T KNOW THAT. ANYTHING COULD HAVE HAPPENED TO YOU. I KNOW YOU WANT YOUR INDEPENDENCE, DINAH, BUT BEING GROWN UP DOESN'T MEAN YOU CAN JUST IGNORE RESPONSIBILITY.

▽ At the party, she told the others what had happened.

MY MOM'S THE SAME – ALWAYS AT ME. SOMETIMES, I GET SO ANGRY; I CAN'T WAIT UNTIL I'M OLD ENOUGH TO LEAVE HOME.

CAN WE CHANGE THE SUBJECT? WHAT ABOUT MY NEIGHBOR, BEV, JOINING THE WANNA-BES? YOU SHOULD SEE THE NEW CLOTHES SHE HAS.

I DON'T KNOW. WE'VE ALL KNOWN ONE ANOTHER FOR AGES. SHE'D BE AN OUTSIDER.

▽ On the weekend, on the way to Roger's, Todd and Rashid bumped into Alec.

WHO SAYS YOU CAN WALK DOWN HERE? DIDN'T I ALREADY TELL YOUR BROTHER? WE DON'T WANT YOUR TYPE POLLUTING THE NEIGHBORHOOD.

IT'S A PUBLIC ROAD. WE'VE AS MUCH RIGHT TO BE HERE AS YOU HAVE. YOU'RE JUST A RACIST.

LEAVE IT, TODD.

IF I EVER SEE YOU OR YOUR BROTHER AGAIN, THERE'LL BE REAL TROUBLE. I THINK YOU KNOW WHAT I MEAN.

△ The boys understood only too well.

▽ Todd and Rashid told Umran what had happened.

LEAVE ALEC TO ME. IT'S TIME HE LEARNED A LESSON.

WE SHOULD GO TO THE POLICE. THREATENING PEOPLE WITH KNIVES IS A VERY SERIOUS CRIME.

WHAT ARE YOU GOING TO DO, UMRAN? FIGHTING WON'T SOLVE ANYTHING. YOU COULD END UP IN A LOT OF TROUBLE.

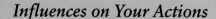

FACTFILE:
PREJUDICE & DISCRIMINATION

Dislike or hatred of a person or group of people based on a preformed and usually false belief is called prejudice. Although it is wrong, prejudice is not in itself a crime. However, if you then treat people unfairly because of your prejudice, this is known as discrimination, and many forms of discrimination are against the law. Racism is one sort of prejudice, which has motivated many crimes — some violent. Racism and all other forms of discrimination need to be challenged. Everyone has the right to live in safety. Perhaps if people took the time to get to know one another, this kind of crime would stop.

WHEN ALEC THREATENS THE BOYS WITH A KNIFE, HE IS COMMITTING A SERIOUS CRIMINAL OFFENSE.

These days we see, hear, and read about crime and violence all the time. The news is filled with different reports. Some people worry that TV and films are also too explicit in what they show and believe that this can influence young people's behavior. However, you should remember that violence you see on-screen is not real and should not be copied.

THE EVENING OF THE PARTY, DINAH'S MOM DIDN'T KNOW WHERE DINAH WAS.

It's normal for young people to want to express their growing independence. This may be through the way they behave or how they dress. Sometimes this behavior can put you at risk, as Dinah's did. Although Dinah didn't get into trouble this time, another time she might not be as lucky.

–5– *Peer Group Pressure*

"I really didn't want to do it, but everyone was staring at me, and I didn't want to look like a coward. All that bothered me was what people would think if I chickened out."

As you go through life, you will form many different relationships. Some of these will last a long time. Others will not. Friends are important for most people. During the years you are at school, you will not only be making friends, you will also be learning how to get along with people of your own peer group — people of a similar age. You will have many things in common but will also be developing your own individual personality.

It is important not to let your own desire to impress friends, and do the kinds of things they do, lead you into trouble.

Your personality will be shaped by how you respond to ideas and situations and how you are affected by peer group pressure — the opinions and persuasive tactics of other people. People of the same age often experience rivalries. For instance, many young people like to be up-to-date with fashion. If your friend has the latest designer label, you might want it too. But remember that you are who you are because of your personality and not your clothes. Many young people hurry to try out new things, especially if they think they will impress others. It's always important to think for yourself.

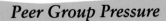

▽ A week later, Dinah said Bev couldn't join the Wanna-bes.

I DON'T GET IT, DINAH. BEV WOULD BE GREAT IN THE GANG. WHY WON'T YOU LET HER JOIN?

YOU'RE TAKING THIS GANG THING TOO SERIOUSLY. WE JUST WANT TO BE FRIENDS.

WE ALL AGREED. ANYWAY, THE GANG WAS MY IDEA IN THE FIRST PLACE, AND I DECIDE WHO'S IN IT.

▽ Bev overheard them.

NO PROBLEM. THIS GANG STUFF'S A BIT TAME FOR MY LIKING ANYWAY, AND YOUR FRIEND OBVIOUSLY CAN'T HANDLE THE COMPETITION.

WHAT COMPETITION? YOU MUST BE JOKING. IT TAKES MORE THAN MONEY AND FLASHY CLOTHES TO IMPRESS ME, YOU KNOW!

▽ The following weekend, Todd & Rashid were on their way to meet Dean.

WHY ARE YOU STILL HANGING AROUND WITH HIM? HE'S A BAD INFLUENCE. LAST TIME TODD ENDED UP STEALING FROM THAT SHOP.

DEAN'S COOL, TODD. HE'S GOT A GIRLFRIEND, YOU KNOW.

YEAH, WELL, IT DEPENDS IF YOU BELIEVE HIM. HE'S SO FULL OF STORIES. COME ON, WE'LL BE LATE.

▽ The group met in the local shopping mall.

AT LAST! WE THOUGHT YOU WEREN'T COMING. LET'S GET SOME BOOZE. I KNOW A STORE WHERE WE CAN GET SOME.

WE'RE TOO YOUNG TO BUY ALCOHOL. THE STORE WOULD BE BREAKING THE LAW SELLING IT TO US.

SO? THE REAL PROBLEM IS WE DON'T HAVE ANY MONEY.

△ Dean noticed an elderly man on a bench. His wallet was sticking out of his back pocket.

I BET IF YOU WERE REALLY QUICK, YOU COULD GET THAT WALLET WITHOUT ANYONE NOTICING.

NO WAY. THINK OF SOMETHING ELSE. I'M NOT A THIEF.

NO, JUST A WIMP. WE DARE YOU TO DO IT.

STOP IT, ALL OF YOU. THAT'S NOT FAIR.

△ The boys kept pressuring him. Eventually Todd gave in to them.

I CAN'T BELIEVE HE DID IT!

NOR ME. COME ON, LET'S CATCH UP WITH HIM.

WHY DID I LISTEN TO THEM? I'VE JUST STOLEN THAT WALLET.

△ Todd went to give Dean the money.

FACTFILE: RESISTING PEER GROUP PRESSURE

Here are some points to remember:
- If you don't want to do something, say so firmly but not aggressively. Make "I" statements: say things like "I won't do that" rather than "We shouldn't do that."
- Don't let others' comments get to you. You aren't being a coward. It takes courage to say no.
- If people make threats, talk to someone you can trust.
- If you know something is against the law, you do not have to do it, no matter what anyone says.

DEAN BOASTED THAT HE HAD A GIRLFRIEND.

If you've ever boasted about something you've done, you might have exaggerated the story. In the same way, the things that friends claim to have done might not be true. So never feel pressured to do something just because your friends say they have done it — whether it's having a girlfriend or boyfriend or committing a crime, like shoplifting.

DEAN DARED TODD TO STEAL THE WALLET, AND THE OTHERS ENCOURAGED HIM.

Sometimes young people dare one another to do something risky or illegal. The person being dared may feel that he or she has to accept the challenge to avoid losing friends. Yet if anyone is using a dare to make you do something you do not want to do, you should say no. A true friend will not use this tactic. If you encourage someone to commit an offense, you may be breaking the law yourself.

− 6 − Drugs and Alcohol

Alcohol and drugs are increasingly a factor in many crimes. Buying alcohol under age or possessing illegal drugs are criminal offenses. These substances interfere with the workings of the body and also affect mental and emotional processes. In some cases people may not know what they are doing, and this has led to situations becoming out of control.

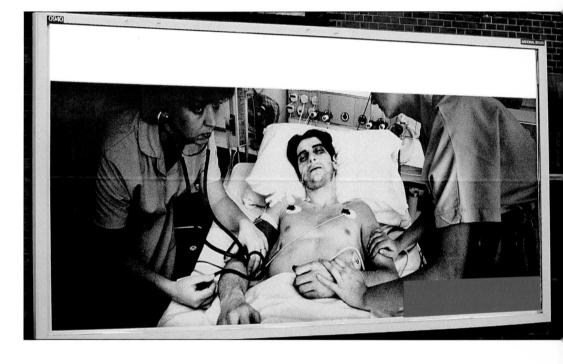

If you are tempted to take drugs, or have already tried them, you should understand the dangers you are exposing yourself to.

Crimes committed under the influence of drugs or alcohol are often spur-of-the-moment ones. Fans at a sport match who have been drinking may become rowdy, and rivalries between different supporters can spill over into fighting. Drugs can alter your thinking about what is real and not. This in turn stops you from being able to tell — or care about — the difference between right and wrong. As you grow up, the desire to experiment and try new things is perfectly natural. You need to think very carefully, however, about the possible consequences of your decisions. There are many people and organizations that can advise you if you need help with a drug or alcohol problem.

▽ An hour later they were all in the park.

> I FEEL AWFUL ABOUT WHAT I JUST DID. THERE ARE DOCUMENTS AND PHOTOS IN HERE TOO. I'M SURE THIS STUFF'S REALLY IMPORTANT TO THAT MAN.

> DON'T WORRY ABOUT IT. THERE WAS MORE MONEY IN THERE THAN WE THOUGHT. I RAN INTO THIS GUY I KNOW AND GOT HIM TO SELL ME THIS.

> WOW, IS THAT A JOINT?

▽ It was. Dean, Eddie, and Rashid tried it. Roger and Todd didn't.

> I FEEL A BIT SICK.

> SERVES YOU RIGHT. YOU SHOULDN'T BE DOING THAT. I'M GOING. I SHOULD NEVER HAVE LISTENED TO YOU ALL.

> YOU DIDN'T HAVE TO. YOU'RE THE ONE WHO BROKE THE LAW. NOW YOU'RE PRETENDING TO BE SOME KIND OF SAINT.

> YOU BROKE THE LAW TOO. YOU KNEW THAT MONEY WAS STOLEN. YOU'D BETTER BE CAREFUL, RASHID. SMOKING THAT DRUG IS ILLEGAL.

△ The dope and alcohol had gone to Rashid's head, and before they knew it, they were having it out.

▽ That evening, Dinah went to Zoe's birthday party.

> NICE PRESENT. I SAW THOSE AT THE MALL. WEREN'T THEY ON CLEARANCE? REJECTS OR SOMETHING?

> VERY FUNNY. SO, WHAT DID YOU GET HER? WAS IT GOLD PLATED?

> DO YOU TWO MIND? BEV'S REALLY OKAY, DINAH. AND GUESS WHAT! SHE'S GOT SOME ECSTASY.

> YOU'VE GOT TO BE JOKING. DON'T YOU LISTEN TO THE NEWS? DRUGS AREN'T MY SCENE. I DON'T NEED THEM TO HAVE A GOOD TIME.

> YOU'RE DRINKING BEER – WHAT DO YOU THINK ALCOHOL IS?

> DON'T BE SUCH A KILLJOY, DINAH. COME ON. IT'LL BE FUN. JUST ONCE CAN'T HURT.

△ Dinah felt that she didn't want to get into drugs.

> OF COURSE IT CAN. PEOPLE HAVE DIED THE FIRST TIME THEY TRIED CERTAIN DRUGS. ANYWAY, CARRYING ECSTASY AND GIVING IT TO SOMEONE ELSE IS A SERIOUS CRIMINAL OFFENSE. IS THIS THE KIND OF THING YOU WANT TO GET INTO?

> DON'T LISTEN TO HER, ZOE. SHE'S JUST AFRAID OF TAKING A RISK.

△ Dinah said that kind of risk just wasn't worth taking.

CASE STUDY:

FATIMA, AGE 14

"I'd never tried alcohol before. I was with some friends. I didn't want to be the only one not drinking. It tasted strange at first. I started laughing and saying stupid things. What frightened me afterward was how out of control I was. The next day, I could only remember half the things we did. Alcohol changed the way I felt, and it was scary how difficult it was to make sense of what I was doing."

UNDER THE INFLUENCE OF ALCOHOL AND DOPE, RASHID WAS AGGRESSIVE TOWARD TODD.

The use of violence against another person is itself a crime. Abuse of drugs and alcohol has been shown to be a significant factor in many different crimes that have also involved violence. In some people this abuse also causes intense feelings and severe mood swings. This means that even those who wouldn't normally use violence can become aggressive once under their influence.

SOME PEOPLE COMMIT CRIMES TO PAY FOR A DRUG OR ALCOHOL HABIT.

Some drugs are very expensive to buy, and suppliers will often hike the prices up as a person becomes more dependent upon them. People have stolen money from others or taken valuable items to get money for drugs. They may have threatened or actually used violence to do this. Some have even turned to prostitution to earn money to buy the drugs they need.

-7- Gangs

Being part of a group can make you feel like you belong, that people you respect have accepted you. Being with people with similar interests allows you to share your thoughts and feelings. Gangs can be different, though. Belonging to a gang isn't a crime, but they can often attract people who want to feel powerful or who enjoy making trouble. This can make gangs dangerous.

Being part of a gang can be good. It is important, however, to decide how far you will go along with what your group does.

Some young people believe that belonging to a particular gang will improve their standing with their friends. Gangs often demand loyalty from their members and may make people undergo an "initiation" before they are allowed to join, to show they are "worthy." In many cases, this has involved someone being expected to commit a crime. The pressures on you to go along with what you are being asked to do can be very strong. If you are in a gang yourself, you might want to think about the kinds of things you do together. Are you at risk of breaking the law? If you are, you should look carefully at why you want to be a member. Sometimes the benefits are not worth the possible consequences.

Gangs

▽ A few days later, Dinah ran into Jill after school.

> HI. WHAT'S SHE DOING HERE? I THOUGHT WE WERE ALL GOING TO THE MOVIES?

> WELL, IF THAT'S THE BEST YOU CAN COME UP WITH, I'M NOT SURPRISED THE OTHERS HAVE DECIDED NOT TO BOTHER WITH THE WANNA-BES ANYMORE.

> BEV! WE HAVEN'T SAID ANYTHING YET.

> WELL, THAT GANG THING WAS PRETTY LAME. WE'RE ALL TOO GROWN UP FOR THAT.

> OH, I SEE. THANKS FOR HAVING THE GUTS TO TELL ME YOURSELF, JILL. IT'S GOOD TO KNOW YOU CAN RELY ON YOUR FRIENDS.

> DINAH, I'M SORRY. I DIDN'T KNOW WHAT TO SAY. BEV'S RIGHT, THOUGH. WHY DO WE NEED A GANG? CAN'T WE ALL JUST HAVE A GOOD TIME?

△ Dinah said she wouldn't join Bev if they begged her, and walked away.

▽ A week later, Todd found out Rashid had been injured on his way home from school.

> THAT'S TERRIBLE. LAST TIME I SAW HIM HE LASHED OUT AT ME – HE WAS REALLY OUT OF IT.

> HE AND UMRAN ARE BOTH BEING REALLY SECRETIVE. I THINK SOMETHING'S GOING ON.

> I KNOW. HE TOLD ME. LOOK, TODD, DO YOU HAVE ANY IDEA WHAT MIGHT HAVE HAPPENED? RASHID'S ARM'S BROKEN, AND HE HAS SOME CUTS AND BRUISES. HE SAYS HE WAS CLIMBING AND FELL, BUT I DON'T THINK HE'S TELLING THE TRUTH.

> I'VE AN AWFUL FEELING IT MIGHT HAVE SOMETHING TO DO WITH ALEC. YOU KNOW HOW HE'S ALWAYS MAKING RACIST COMMENTS. WELL, HE THREATENED THE TWO OF US A WHILE BACK. I THINK HE AND UMRAN HAVE SOME KIND OF GRUDGE THING GOING ON.

△ Todd thought Alec might have hurt Rashid to get at Umran.

▽ That afternoon in town, Bev saw Dinah and began to taunt her.

> DINAH, ALL ON YOUR OWN, I SEE. WHAT A SHAME. WELL, WHAT SHOULD WE DO TONIGHT, GIRLS?

> BEV, DON'T BE ROTTEN.

> I'M SICK OF THIS. WHO DOES SHE THINK SHE IS?

▽ Dinah suddenly lost control, and she and Bev began to fight. As they struggled, they didn't look where they were going.

> HEY, WATCH OUT!

THERE ARE OFTEN RIVALRIES BETWEEN DIFFERENT GANGS. This can sometimes lead to trouble. Gangs might lay claim to a particular area or make rules that other people are expected to obey. Fights between rival gangs are common and have become a problem in some communities. Dinah and Bev's actions could have had serious consequences for themselves or people around them. If they had hurt the child, that would have been a serious offense.

CASE STUDY: THE INITIATION

"I'd been wanting to be a member of this gang at school. Finally the leader agreed that I could join, but only if I did something to prove I was worthy of being in the gang. The leader came up with this crazy stunt he wanted me to do. There was a gap between two buildings where we lived, and I had to jump across it. It wasn't far, but if I hadn't made the jump, the drop would have killed me. I didn't do it. The gang had it out with me, but I was glad I didn't get into the gang, if that's the kind of stuff they did."

DECIDING TO TELL ON SOMEONE IS NOT EASY TO DO. Some people believe that loyalty to friends and family comes above everything. Others think if you have information that could solve a crime, you should tell someone, no matter who's involved. If you do not speak out when you know someone is going to commit a crime, not only are you involving yourself, you are missing the chance to stop them from getting into serious trouble.

8

Crime and Punishment

"It was when I found myself in the police station with everyone treating me like a criminal that I realized just how stupid I'd been."

As you know, a crime is any action or failure to act that breaks a law. Laws are made by the government of each country and can be altered to reflect changes in society's needs and attitudes. They are there to protect you and to safeguard the basic rights of every person. The law also lays down the procedures and punishments for those who break them. The legal system is designed to be as fair as possible, but that does not mean it is an easy or pleasant experience to become involved in the legal process.

Someone who has admitted to a crime, or whom the police reasonably suspect of having committed one, will be arrested. What happens afterward will depend on the age of the person and the offense he or she is accused of committing. People may be held in custody until they appear in court, especially if the police think they may be dangerous. In court, both sides will give evidence, and depending on the type of case, the evidence will be considered by either a judge or jury. If someone is found guilty, the judge will decide on a suitable punishment. Anyone arrested on suspicion of a crime has specific rights that the police must respect. If you were ever to be in this situation, you should cooperate with the police and take advantage of these rights.

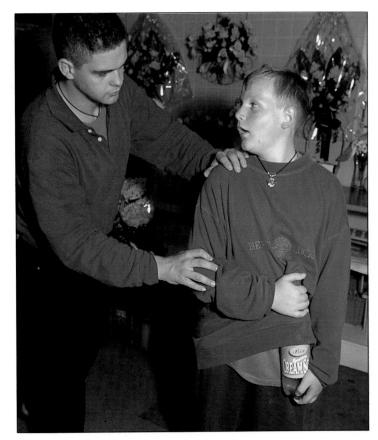

Even if you feel that laws don't apply to you, if caught, you will have to go through the legal system.

▽ When Dinah returned home, she felt miserable.

DINAH, WHAT HAPPENED TO YOU? YOU LOOK TERRIBLE. WHY IS YOUR SHIRT TORN? HAVE YOU BEEN FIGHTING?

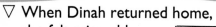

MOM, I'M NOT IN THE MOOD TO ARGUE WITH YOU RIGHT NOW. SOMETHING AWFUL HAPPENED.

▽ Dinah started crying and told her mom what had happened.

I JUST LOST CONTROL. YOU SHOULD HAVE SEEN THAT WOMAN. SHE WAS SO ANGRY. WE MANAGED TO STOP THE BABY CARRIAGE FROM FALLING, AND THE BABY WASN'T HURT, BUT IT COULD HAVE BEEN SO MUCH WORSE.

▽ The following day, Todd came by to see Rashid.

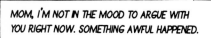

I'M SORRY ABOUT WHAT I SAID. BUT I STILL WISH I'D NEVER GOTTEN INVOLVED WITH DEAN. SO, ARE YOU GOING TO TELL US WHAT HAPPENED?

I WAS JUST FOOLING AROUND. I FELL, THAT'S ALL.

YOU DON'T HAVE TO LIE TO US, RASHID. TODD TOLD ME ABOUT THE THREATS ALEC MADE. DID HE DO THIS TO YOU?

YEAH. BUT YOU CAN'T SAY ANYTHING. YOU DON'T KNOW ALEC. HE'S NOT JUST A RACIST OR A BULLY. I THINK HE GETS A KICK OUT OF HURTING PEOPLE. IF HIS BROTHER HADN'T BEEN THERE WITH ME . . .

WHAT? ROGER WAS THERE? BUT HE HASN'T MENTIONED ANYTHING.

I'M NOT SURPRISED. HE'S AS FRIGHTENED AS ANYONE. ALEC ROUGHED HIM UP TOO WHEN HE TRIED TO STOP HIM FROM HITTING ME.

I KNOW, BUT I'M SCARED TO SAY ANYTHING. ALEC THREATENED TO DO SOMETHING WORSE IF I TOLD ANYONE BUT UMRAN. IT WAS MEANT AS A WARNING, TO STOP UMRAN AND HIS FRIENDS FROM GOING INTO ALEC'S NEIGHBORHOOD.

RASHID, WE HAVE TO TELL MOM AND DAD AND CALL THE POLICE.

WELL, WE HAVE TO DO SOMETHING. WHAT ALEC DID TO YOU IS A SERIOUS CRIME. WE CAN'T JUST LET HIM GET AWAY WITH IT.

▽ The next day, Todd was surprised by a visit from the police.

WHAT'S THIS ABOUT? IS IT RASHID?

NO, THESE PEOPLE ARE HERE TO SEE YOU.

TWO WEEKS AGO, A GENTLEMAN HAD HIS WALLET STOLEN IN THE SHOPPING MALL. THE THIEF WAS CAUGHT ON THE SECURITY VIDEO CAMERAS, AND YOU'VE BEEN IDENTIFIED AS THE PERSON ON THE VIDEO.

▽ Todd was arrested. He then spent an hour in a cell at the police station and was interviewed.

YOU WERE SEEN COMMITTING A SERIOUS OFFENSE. WE HAVE YOU ON CAMERA TAKING A WALLET. WE'D LIKE YOU TO MAKE A STATEMENT ABOUT WHAT YOU DID.

I DIDN'T MEAN TO DO ANYTHING. I'M REALLY SORRY. IT WAS A DARE.

TELL US WHAT HAPPENED, TODD – THE TRUTH, MIND YOU. THEN WE CAN ALL GO HOME.

▽ Todd admitted to the crime. He said the friends he was with had encouraged him.

IT WAS STUPID. I DIDN'T WANT TO DO IT.

WHO WERE YOU WITH, TODD?

THIS IS VERY SERIOUS, TODD. YOU DO REALIZE THAT YOUR FRIENDS WERE ALSO COMMITTING AN OFFENSE BY ENCOURAGING YOU TO STEAL THE WALLET, DON'T YOU? THINK ABOUT IT SERIOUSLY, TODD.

▽ Todd told them about Dean and Eddie. He and his dad waited while the police decided what to do.

WE HAVE DECIDED TO WARN YOU FOR THIS OFFENSE, TODD – BECAUSE YOU HAVEN'T BEEN IN TROUBLE BEFORE. BUT IF WE SEE YOU HERE AGAIN, YOU WON'T GET AWAY WITH A WARNING – UNDERSTAND?

YES, I UNDERSTAND. I'M SORRY.

DON'T WORRY. HE WON'T BE IN HERE AGAIN.

▽ That night, Todd's parents asked him why he'd done what he did.

I WAS BEING DARED INTO IT, AND I DIDN'T WANT TO LOOK LIKE A COWARD.

THAT'S NO EXCUSE, TODD. YOU DO REALIZE THAT THIS WILL GO ON YOUR RECORD? A WARNING'S NOT SOMETHING TO TAKE LIGHTLY.

I CAN'T UNDERSTAND WHY YOU'D DO SOMETHING LIKE THAT, TODD.

I WAS STUPID, AND I'M REALLY SORRY. THE WALLET'S IN MY ROOM. THE MONEY'S GONE, BUT THERE WERE DOCUMENTS AND STUFF I COULDN'T THROW AWAY. HE'D PROBABLY WANT THEM.

△ Mr. Schaeffer said he'd take the wallet to the police the next day.

THE POLICE HAVE ARRESTED TODD.

The police are there to prevent crime and to catch criminals. If they have enough cause to suspect someone of having broken the law, they can arrest that person and question him or her. If you are ever stopped by the police, whether or not you have done anything wrong, it is important that you do not try to resist or run away.

TODD NOW HAS A CRIMINAL RECORD.

If anyone is convicted of a crime, a note of the conviction will be kept on file forever. Having a criminal record may mean people doubt your honesty and feel uneasy with you or that you won't be able to get the job you want. It could affect you throughout your life.

DEAN KNEW THE MONEY WAS STOLEN.

Although he did not steal the wallet, he has committed a crime by encouraging Todd and

could be held just as responsible as Todd. If you take any part in a crime, whether or not you played an active role, you could be prosecuted. Those who are accessories to a crime may receive the same punishment as the person who committed the crime.

9

Staying Legal

"I'm glad I didn't go along with the others. I knew what they were doing was wrong, and I felt good for having stood up for what I felt was right."

Although crime has always been part of society and will probably be present for a long time to come, there is a great deal you can do to make sure that you do not let yourself become a part of the problem. You may already have decided that you will never do anything to break the law, and that is a very important first step. But it is also vital to remain aware of potential risk situations and not to let yourself be persuaded by outside factors to do things you know, or believe, are wrong.

There are many ways to enjoy yourself without getting into trouble.

People might talk about the "buzz" of committing a crime or may tell you that the law is unfair and therefore it's okay to break it. Some laws may even seem wrong to you, but that does not give anyone the right to commit an offense. Laws vary from country to country, but most are created to protect people's rights and property. Finding out about the law and your rights under it will help you to be clear about what is a crime and what isn't and will help you to avoid situations that could be problematic.

▽ One night after school, Jill caught up with Dinah.

CAN WE TALK? LOOK, I NEVER WANTED TO FALL OUT WITH YOU. TO BE HONEST, BEV'S A BIT BORING. ALL SHE'S GOT IS MONEY, AND WE'RE ALL SICK OF HER FLASHING THAT AROUND.

I SHOULDN'T HAVE LET HER GET TO ME. MIND YOU, SHE WAS RIGHT ABOUT THE GANG IDEA. IT WAS STUPID.

▽ Rashid and Shobu knew about Todd's arrest.

WE HAVEN'T TOLD ANYONE. WHAT HAPPENED WITH THE POLICE?

IT WAS AWFUL. I WAS PUT IN A CELL. THEY GAVE ME A WARNING, AND I TOLD THEM WHAT HAPPENED.

I WISH WE'D NEVER MET DEAN. ALL THIS IS HIS FAULT.

I'M THE ONE WHO STOLE THAT WALLET. DEAN BROKE THE LAW BY SHOPLIFTING AND SUPPLYING DRUGS, BUT I DIDN'T HAVE TO DO THE SAME. I HAD A CHOICE. AND NOW IT FEELS LIKE NO ONE TRUSTS ME ANYMORE.

▷ Todd told them that the warning meant that he now had a criminal record.

▽ Dean himself had had a visit from the police. He was angry with Todd.

THANKS TO YOU, I'M GOING TO GET AT LEAST A SECOND WARNING. YOU GOT ME INTO A LOT OF TROUBLE.

YOU'RE THE ONE WHO STARTED ALL THIS. I DIDN'T KNOW YOU'D BEEN WARNED ALREADY. AND I DIDN'T TELL THE POLICE EVERYTHING I KNOW. YOU'D BETTER BE CAREFUL IN FUTURE.

▽ Later, Todd told Rashid that Alec had been arrested.

HE GOT INTO A FIGHT AND PULLED A KNIFE. YOU SHOULD TELL THE POLICE ABOUT HIM ATTACKING YOU. I THINK ROGER MIGHT BE MORE WILLING TO SPEAK OUT NOW TOO.

I AM GOING TO TELL THEM; I SPOKE TO DAD AND UMRAN LAST NIGHT.

▽ Several weeks later, Todd and his friends were in the park.

WHAT'S WRONG, TODD?

YOU'VE LEARNED YOUR LESSON, THOUGH.

I WAS JUST THINKING ABOUT WHAT HAPPENED. I NEVER THOUGHT I'D END UP WITH A CRIMINAL RECORD. I'M NEVER GOING TO DO ANYTHING AS STUPID AS THAT AGAIN.

TODD IS SORRY THAT HE GOT INVOLVED WITH DEAN.

It is sometimes easy to forget to consider the consequences of your actions, either immediately or later in life. When you are young, especially, it can seem as though the future is so far away that nothing you do now could possibly affect it. It is important to remember that the actions and decisions you make as you grow up can all have a significant effect on your life.

FACTFILE: IT'S UP TO YOU

Whether you become involved in crime is up to you. It has to be your responsibility in the end. Although it can be hard to stand up and say no to someone, or to give up what might appear to be a solution to a difficult problem, it is worth it. The effect on your life of getting into trouble or crime can be long-lasting and may prove devastating in the end.

TODD COOPERATED WHEN HE WAS INTERVIEWED BY THE POLICE.

If you're ever stopped by a police officer, stay calm and find out the reason. To arrest you, the police must have enough cause to suspect a crime has been or is about to be committed. Even if you know you are innocent, cooperate. You'll have the chance to prove your innocence, but you could be breaking the law by refusing to do what the police say. Finding out what your rights are regarding lawyers, having parents present, and who you can talk to is a good idea. The police should also tell you these things — don't be afraid to ask. The police enforce the law, but they also have to obey it.

—10— What Can We Do?

"I hated rules and regulations. All my friends used to say they hated them too. After a while, I began to realize that most are there for a good reason — for everyone's protection."

Crime causes a lot of pain and upset to many people. You will know that becoming a criminal will not help you to escape from problems or impress others. You will understand more about the reasons people can find themselves getting into trouble or committing crimes. By understanding this, you can make sure you stay on the right side of the law.

Talking about concerns or worries with people close to you can often help to solve a problem.

If you have been tempted to become involved with crime, or have already committed an offense, you should think carefully about your actions and the effects they could have on your life and that of others. If you have a problem, talking about it to someone you trust can help. Remember that it's never too late to decide to ask for help. In addition, there are many organizations that will offer support. If you are in trouble, talk to someone before you find yourself caught up in more serious situations. Don't forget that it is never too late to get advice and guidance, even if you are already involved in crime.

Adults and young people who have read this book together might want to discuss their ideas about the issues raised. Anyone who would like to talk to someone not directly involved about any aspect of crime should be able to obtain advice and support from the organizations listed below.

CENTER FOR COMMUNITY ALTERNATIVES
115 East Jefferson Street
Suite 300
Syracuse, NY 13202
(315) 422-5638

NATIONAL YOUTH GANG CENTER (NYGC)
Institute for Intergovernmental Research
P.O. Box 12729
Tallahassee, FL 32317
(800) 446-0912
http://www.iir.com/nyge

YOUTH CRIME WATCH OF AMERICA
9300 South Dadeland Boulevard
Suite 100
Miami, FL 33156
(305) 670-2409
http://www.ycwa.org

NATIONAL CONSORTIUM ON ALTERNATIVES FOR YOUTH AT RISK (NCAYAR)
5250 17th Street
Suite 107
Sarasota, FL 34235-8247
(800) 245-7133
http://www.ncayar.org

TEENS AGAINST GANG VIOLENCE
2 Moody Street
Dorchester, MA 02124
(617) 282-9659
http://tagv.org

VOICES FOR CHILDREN
180 Dundas Street West
Suite 1900
Toronto, Ontario
Canada M5G 1Z8
(800) 321-1078
http://www.voices4children.org

Index

Photocredits
All the pictures in this book are by Roger Vlitos, apart from the following pages: 1, 13 top, & 23 top — Frank Spooner Pictures; 7 top, 10 bottom, 17, 19 top, & 26 bottom — Rex Features. The publishers wish to acknowledge that all the people photographed in this book are models.